PRICE MATTERS

Factors Influencing the Price of Gold, Silver, Crude Oil, Copper and Platinum

- By Julian Sanders

Table of Content

Chapter Four

Chapter Five

Conclusion   34

INTRODUCTION

Investments in gold, silver, platinum, copper and crude oil around the world have become increasingly profitable over the years. These natural resources now constitute hot spots for profitable investments. Hence, most investors now wish to include one or more of these in their portfolio. However, investing or trading in one or more of these natural resources does not guarantee automatic profit. To be a successful investor or trader in this field, you need to be skilled, diligent, smart and well informed.

Being well informed means that you must be equipped with adequate information about how things roll in the natural resources market. This information will serve has your guide for making wise and professional decisions when trading. Some of the most important information that you need to be a successful trader are those relating to factors influencing the price of gold, silver, platinum, copper and oil. The price of these commodities at a given point in time is influenced by various economic and non-economic factors. Studying and understanding these factors will help you make professional decisions as to when to trade and how to trade in any of these commodities. The price of each of these commodities is very volatile. It has the tendency to change on a daily basis. Thus, predicting changes in the price of these commodities can be very complex. However, you can always get your way when you have a firm grasp of the underlying price drivers of these commodities.

The aim of this book is to help you improve your trade by providing you with necessary information and description on factors influencing the price of gold, silver, platinum, copper and oil in the world. We shall provide you with information on basic macro-economic factors that drive the price of each of these commodities bit by bit as the book proceeds. We hope that you
will have an amazing time reading through the book.

Chapter One

Factors Affecting the Price of Gold

For centuries, gold has maintained its status has a reliable tool for storing value. Its purchasing power is relatively stable and it has proven itself to be a reliable tool for saving and investment. Gold is undoubtedly considered to be a highly valuable asset that can endure the fragility and instability of the world economic system. It is generally referred to as a safe haven investment. Hence, it is a big time investment for the government as well has private investors around the world. Millions of people around the world have made huge amount of money in gold investment. Moreover, it is one of the important commodities in the world macro-economic space.

As hinted earlier, gold is a safe haven investment. However, making profit from any investment or trading related to gold demands measurable professional efforts and skills. One of the skills required is related to knowing how the factors affecting the price of gold works. In this light, let us discuss some of the factors affecting the price of gold in the world.

(A) Demand and Supply

This is the major factor affecting the price of gold; that is, other factors relate to it in one way or the other. Just like any other goods, the relationship between demand and supply, to a large extent, determine the price of gold. When the supply is higher than demand, the price reduces and while the demand is higher than supply, the price will increase. However, in the gold market, the demand is usually higher than the supply. So, the main question is "how high is the demand?" This means that demand has more influence on the price of gold.

Generally, demands for gold can be broadly categorized into three: jewelry demands, investment demands, industrial demands and demands from central banks.

(i)   Jewelry Demands

This represents the demand of gold by jewelry manufacturing companies in other to manufacture gold jewelries. The demand for gold by jewelry companies is usually high. Researches reveal it that demands for gold covers up to 68% percent of the total demand for gold. Jewelry demands for gold come from all part of the world. However, a larger part of the demands come from India and China. Indians are known for using gold jewelries for wedding gifts and festival offerings, and religious activities. Hence, the price of gold is usually high during Indian festive periods and religious holiday as activities of these periods usually automatically result into a large increase in the general demand for gold. Also, the price of gold usually increases during Chinese long New Year festival. Generally, the demand for gold around the world is usually high during festive seasons such as Christmas season and New Year festivals. Knowing this, you should be able to predict that the price of gold will rise during these periods.

(ii)   Investment Demands

This accounts for demands for gold from different parts of the world for the purpose of investment. As hinted earlier, gold is a reliable tool for saving and investment. Investors buy gold when its price is low and sell it when it is high to amass huge profits. The rate of the demand for gold for investment is not stable as it is largely determined by other macro- economic factors such as dollar exchange rate, interest rate, inflation rate, silver price and oil price. When the demand of gold by investor is high the price of gold per ounce will automatically rise and when investors demand less its price per ounce will fall.

(iii)   Demands by Central Banks.

A commendable amount of the demand for gold also comes from central banks around. Gold is a global inflation hedger. It hedging status has proven it to be a sure instrument for saving and insuring currency devaluation. Unlike fiat currencies, the purchasing power of gold is enduring and is

Usually relatively stable during economic struggles. Thus, it is common for central banks to keep gold in their foreign reserve to serve as an insurance against currency devaluation. During periods of world economic instabilities the demand for gold by central banks is always high, thereby causing a rise in the price of gold.

(iv)   Industrial Demands

It account for the demand for gold by manufacturing and medical industries. Gold is usually demanded by medical industries especially dental purposes. For instance, it is used to produce golden teeth in order to meet the demands of Muslim pilgrims who purchase and use golden tooth as a holy relics from Mecca in Saudi Arabia. Industrial demand for gold has rapidly increasing as a result of new developments in technology. Gold is now being used in nanotechnology, electronic devices and chemical processes.

The rate of demands for gold usually has more influence on the price of gold than the rate of the supply of gold. This is as a result of the relative stability in the supply of gold in world market. World gold council (2013) reports that influencing factors affect gold through two channels of supply: mine production and recycled gold.

(i)   Mine Production

Over 60% of gold supply comes from mine production. Bulk of gold supply in the world gold market from gold mining industries comes from world top gold producing countries which include USA, China, Russia, South Africa, Latin America, Australia and Peru. The supply of gold is usually affected by government policies in these countries. When the government policies favor the mining and supply of gold the price of gold may rise or fall depending on the status of other macro-economic factors. This means that a stable gold supply does not have much influence on gold price. The price of gold may become relatively high or low as a result of other macro-

economic factors such as dollar exchange rates, interest rate, crude oil price, inflation, income rates and global economic changes even when the supply is stable. However, there is a high probability for a sky-high increase in the price of gold if government policies cause a decrease in gold mining activities.

(ii)   Recycled Gold

Supply from recycled gold covers a remarkable part of gold supply per year. There is a high tendency for consumers to recycle their golden jewelries or other gold product and sell it when the price of gold is high.

Another reliable gold supply channel is (iii) the monetary sector sales. Supply of gold from the monetary sectors accounts for the sales of gold by central banks and other giant organizations such as IMF (international monetary fund). As mentioned earlier, central banks hold gold in their reserve to store value and insure currency devaluation. Central banks may decide to sell part of their gold reserve when the price of gold is high for economic reasons. The sales of gold by banks are guided by CBGA (Central Banks Gold Agreement) which hold that central banks cannot sell more than 500 tons a year. Supply of gold from this channel involves central banks in Europe and North America.

Having discussed the influence of demand and supply on the price of gold, let us look at other macro-economic factors affecting the price of gold. These include US dollar, interest rate, crude oil price, inflation, consumer's income, and central banks policies. Before we proceed, I want you to note that other factors that will be examined are interrelated and that these factors are significant to changes in the price of gold because they directly influence the demand for gold.

(B) US Dollar

Us dollar is the world leading currency. It is the global reserve currency. As such, changes in the value of dollar usually influence the price of gold. Whenever dollar depreciates, there will be a sky-high increase in gold
demand. Gold price has a negative correlation with the value of US dollar;

8

that is, a decrease in the value of dollar is not equal to a decrease in the price of gold. Rather, the price of gold increases when the value of dollar decreases. The purchasing power of gold is enduring and cannot be easily affected by macro-economic factors influencing the value of dollar. In this light, investors and central banks demands for more gold when dollar depreciates in order to store value. Consequently, this increase in demand usually leads to a remarkable increase in the price of gold.

(C) Interest Rates

Interest rates have been identified to be one of the leading factors that determine the rise and fall of gold price. On the one hand, when interest rates are high, investors are likely to focus more on short-term interest paying investments, thereby leaving the gold investment space. This is because interest paying investments yield faster than gold which is a long- term investment. This automatically results into a decrease in gold demands. As such, the price of gold usually falls when the interest rates are high. On the other hand, when the interest rates are low, investors would leave interest paying investment and invest more on gold. This definitely increases the demand for gold and keeps its price soaring higher.

(D) Inflation

The common effect of inflation is to decrease the purchasing power of currencies. Gold has been identified by economic analyst to be a reliable instrument for hedging inflation as the purchasing power of gold is relatively stable. As such during inflation, central banks and investors opt for the purchase of gold in other to store value. These activities relate to the fact the purchasing power of fiat currencies can be protected by converting them into gold whose purchasing value is relatively stable irrespective of inflation.

(E) Consumer Income

Consumer income is one of the major determining factors of gold price. As discussed earlier, the demand of gold for jewelries production covers about
68% of the total demand for gold. The demand for gold by jewelry industries
at any given time is greatly influenced by the level of consumer income. The

demand for gold automatically increases when there is an increase in the disposable income of the consumers. Consumers only demand for jewelries after their primary needs have been satisfied; that is, consumers demand for jewelries when they have abundance. Therefore, when consumer income rates are high the price of gold will increase while the price of gold will decrease when consumer income rates are low.

(F) Crude Oil Price

There is a positive correlation between the price of crude oil and that of gold. An increase in crude oil price will lead to an increase in gold price. Increase in crude oil price is one of those factors that can trigger inflation. When the purchasing price of crude oil increases, the purchasing price of paper money will generally decrease. Consequently, investors and banks will have to invest in gold which is a reliable inflation hedging tool in other to safeguard value. This automatically increases the demand for gold, thus leading to an increase in gold price.

(G) Central Banks Policies

Lastly, central banks policies are significant to the gold price. About 20% percent of the world gold is held by central banks around the world. As such, central banks policies on the sale and purchase of gold have a profound influence of the price of gold in the world gold market. When central banks policies favor more demand, the price of gold will appreciate and when it does not, the price of gold may decrease relatively.

In conclusion, understanding the status of the above macro-economic factors influencing the price of gold at a given point in time will contribute greatly to your success as an investor or trader. It is also important that you update yourself on daily basis with new information on these factors as their status is not stable.

(H) Natural Disasters

Natural disasters involving any of the largest gold producing countries (USA, China, Russia, South Africa, Latin America, Australia and Peru) can lead to a decrease in the supply of gold. Natural disasters such as earthquake and landslides may affect gold mines. Consequently, this can lead to an increase in the price of gold.

(I) Mining Strike

Cases of strike in one or more of the gold producing companies in the top gold producing countries will lead to a decrease in the supply of gold in the global market. This can cause a temporal increase in gold scarcity rate, thereby causing the price of gold to increase.

Chapter Two

Factors Influencing the Price of Crude Oil

Crude oil is one of the leading commodities in international macro-economy. Crude oil has a profound influence on global economy. This is as a result of its status as an important source of energy. Both private and public industries, companies and organizations around the world need oil for one or more purposes on daily basis. Oil is also important to transportation as vehicles are powered by crude oil. It is also used for powering various mechanical engines around the world. It is also use for heating homes during winter in Europe. Crude oil remains a primary commodity that affects world's economy. As such, crude oil is a hot commodity and a profitable investment. To be a successful investor in the crude oil market, you need to have a clear understanding of factors affecting the price of crude oil in the world market.

Hence, let us go into a brief discussion of these factors: (A)

Demand and supply

Just like the price of gold, the basic economic concepts of demand and supplies influence the price of crude oil directly. An increase in crude oil demand will result into an increase in the price of crude oil and an increase in gold supply will lead to a decrease in the price of crude oil. That is, there is a positive correlation between the price of oil and the demand for oil. This simply means that an increase in the demand for oil will lead to an increase in the price of crude oil, and vice versa. There is a negative correlation between the price of oil and oil supply; that is, an increase in the supply of oil will lead to a decrease in its price. The demand for crude oil is usually higher than its supply as oil is used in all parts of the world for both industrial and non-industrial applications. The force of demand and supply is the major driver of oil price. Other factors only influence the price of crude oil because of their capacity to affect its demand and supply.

(B) Weather

Weather is one of those factors that affect the demand for crude oil in the world. There is usually an increase in the demand for crude oil during winter and summer. Winter comes the beginning and end of the year. Due to the high decrease of temperature during winter, there is usually an increase in the demand of oil during winter season, especially in Europe as individuals use crude oil for heating their homes. There is also a high tendency for the demand of oil to increase during summer as Americans consume more crude oil in the course of travelling from one country to the other for vacation during summer. Positive changes in crude oil demand during winter and summer vacations will automatically increase the price of crude oil during these seasons.

(C) Organization of Petroleum Exporting Countries (OPEC)

OPEC which is made up of 13 oil producing countries (Algeria, Angola, Ecuador, Indonesia, Iran, Kuwait, Libya, Nigeria, Qatar, Saudi Arabia, Venezuela, Iraq and Libya) controls about 61% of world crude oil supply. As such, OPEC has the power to influence the general supply of oil in the global oil market. OPEC's oil supply is based on a regulated quota system in other to prevent the price of crude oil from falling. OPEC is known for cutting oil supply in order to maintain the price of crude oil. With OPEC quota system based oil supply, the price of oil is usually relatively higher. However, OPEC has recently decided to leave the supply of crude oil unchanged in reaction to the increasing oil supply competition that is being posed by American Shale oil supply. The American shale oil supply remarkably doubled in 2011 and 2014, thereby increasing crude oil supply and reducing the power of OPEC as the major supplier of crude oil. This has also affected the power of OPEC to determine the price of crude oil by cutting supply. Consequently, OPEC decides to leave the supply of crude oil unchanged in order to make the price of crude oil reduce to a point when the American shale oil will be forced out of the crude oil major supplier space. This OPEC's decision in addition to the increase in supply caused by the American shale oil supply, the price of crude has reduced drastically since 2011 till date.

(D) Natural and Artificial Disasters

Natural and artificial disasters can lead to a large decrease in the supply and demand of crude oil, especially when they involve one or more of the top oil producing or oil consuming countries. Natural disasters can cause the destruction of pipelines and refineries. The destruction refineries will automatically lead to a drastic decrease of crude oil supply, thereby causing a sky high increase in the price of crude oil. For instance hurricane Katrina led to a huge increase in the price of crude oil in 2005 as a result of the destruction it caused. During the hurricane, a huge number of offshore oil, gas platforms and pipelines were destroyed. This reportedly affected about

19% of the world crude oil supply. Hence, the price of crude oil soared uncontrollably high in 2005. Moreover, natural disasters can lead to a decrease in oil demand if it affects one or more of the major oil consuming countries.

More so, artificial disasters such as war usually affect the price of oil, especially when it involves major oil producing or consuming countries. The price of crude oil is usually high when there is war or crisis in oil producing countries. For instance, the 1980 Iraq-Iran war lead to a great decrease of oil production in the two countries and a doubling increase in the price of oil.

(E) Oil reserves

Oil consuming and oil producing countries usually have crude oil reserves in order to carter for future increase in the price of fuel. Crude oil reserves are used to hedge inflation when the price of oil increases in the world market. When the price of crude oil is high and its crude oil is scarce, countries will release the oil in their reserves in order to increase the supply of crude oil and reduce it price. In this light, oil reserves help in regulating the price of crude oil.

(F) Technological Changes

Developments in technology have a remarkable influence on the price of crude oil. Technological developments have consistently contributed the oil production capacity in the global economy overtime. With technology, oil production has become easy, faster and less costly. Increase in technological development will result to an increase in the supply of oil and a decrease in the price of crude oil.

Developments in technology guarantee the invention of more mechanical products that requires the use of crude oil. Such invention will generally lead to an increase in the demand of crude oil. Hence, technological developments relating to the invention of petrol powered engines can lead to an increase in the price of crude oil in the global market.

(G)US and China economy

USA is the largest oil consuming country in the world. Therefore, changes in US economy constitute one of the determining factors of oil price in the world. On the one hand, Buoyancy in US economy normally results into an increase in the demand of oil, thereby increasing the price of crude oil in the world crude oil market. On the other hand, negative changes in US economy will relatively result into a decrease in the demand of oil, thereby leading to a decrease in the price of crude oil.

China is the second largest oil consuming country. Thus, changes in china economy as in the case of US economy discussed above usually reflect in the price of crude oil.

(H)Government policies

Government policies around the world can determine the price of oil in the global market. Governments have the power to directly influence oil production and oil reserves. For instance, the government of a particular oil producing country can decide to make policies that will reduce oil drilling and production activities in their states. This will eventually reduce the supply and increase the price of oil in the oil market. Moreover, political instability in large oil producing states will normally lead to a sky high increase in the price of oil. For instance, the 1973 Arab oil Embargo
triggered a sharp rise in the price of crude oil in the global market.

(I) Tax rates

Tax rates constitute one of those factors that affect the cost of oil production and distribution. High tax rates will lead to an increase in the cost of oil production and distribution while low tax rates will lead to a decrease in the cost of oil production and distribution. Tax rates eventually affect the price of oil as the cost of production and distribution is one of those factors that
determine the cost price of oil in the market.

Chapter Three

Factors Influencing the Price of Copper

The value of copper to industries around the world cannot be overemphasized. Owing to its versatility and conductivity, copper happens to be the third world most used metals (following aluminum and iron). It is widely   industries around the world, especially the construction, telecommunication industries and transportation industries. It is widely used for wiring, piping, heating and cooling equipment. It also serves as a source of profit for traders who place speculative bets of the direction of copper in the global market. Like other natural resources, the price of copper is volatile; thus, trader/investors needs to have a better understanding of the factors that that drives the price of copper in order to make informed decisions. Factors influencing the price of copper in the market include the following:

(A)Demand

Demand plays a vital role in determining the price of copper. High demand for copper will lead to an increase in the price of copper, and vice versa. The demand of copper is generally determined by the demand of goods and services that involve the use of copper. For instance when there is an increase in the demand of construction services construction industries will logically demand for more copper which is used for piping and wiring. This will generally increase the demand of copper as well as its price in the global market. More so, an increase in the demand for electronic equipment will lead to an increase in the demand and price of copper.

(B)Supply

There is a negative correlation between the price of copper and the supply of copper. When the supply of copper is high, the price of copper will reduce while the price of copper will increase when there is a decrease in its supply. The supply of copper comes from two different channels: mine production and recycled copper. The mine production supplies are otherwise referred to
as virgin copper supplies. A bulk of the virgin copper supplies come from

America, particularly Chile and Peru. Chile and Peru control about 40% of world copper reserve and about 42% of copper production.

(C) Supply Disruptions

As hinted earlier a larger percentage of the world copper supply comes from South America, particularly Peru and Chile. The economic situation in these countries is quite turbulent. Strikes and labor disputes are very rampant in these regions. This usually results into temporal disruptions in the production and distribution of copper in the market. During these periods of strike and labor dispute, the supply of copper will decrease and the price of copper will shoot up.

(D) Weather

Weather plays a significant role in determining the price of copper as it has a remarkable effect on the demand for copper by construction industries. Cold temperature, snowy or rainy weather can cause a decrease in the demand for copper as industrial demands is usually low during this period, especially in the construction company. This means that the price of copper is normally low during winter and rainy seasons.

(E)Availability of Substitute Metals

Recently, industries now prefer to go for cheaper metals which can be used to replace copper in order to reduce the cost of production. For instance, aluminum is now being used in electrical equipment, power cables, automobile radiators and cooling tubes. Titanium and steel are also used in heat exchangers. The availability and price of substitute metals can result into a decrease in the demand for copper, thus decreasing the price of copper. As such, information relating to the availability of substitute metals considered when trading or investing in copper.

(F) Urbanization

Urbanization has a remarkable influence on the demand for crude oil. Urbanization in emerging markets like China and India paves way for an increase in the demand for construction services. Consequently, urbanization increases the demand for copper by construction industries. In this manner, the price of copper will increase when there is an increase the urban development in these emerging markets. It should be noted that urbanization in China and India is determined by their economy. When there economy is strong urbanization rates will increase, and vice versa.

(G) US and Chinese Economy

The top copper consuming countries are developed industrial countries. Among these countries USA and China happens to be the largest consumers of copper in the world. China is the first in the world copper consumption rank. China consumes about 40% of the world copper. USA ranks the second largest consumer of copper in the world. Owing to this fact, the economy of these two countries has a profound influence on the price of copper in the global market. When there is economic buoyancy in any or both of these countries, the demand for copper and the price of copper will increase relatively. On the contrary, when there are negative changes in the economy of any or both of these countries the demand for copper will fall, thereby, causing a decrease in the price of copper.

It should be noted that the economy of other developed industrial countries such as Japan, Western European Countries and other countries. However, the USA and China economy dominate the control of copper price in the global market because they are the largest consumers.

(H) Cost of Production

There is a positive correlation between the cost of copper production and the price of copper. That is, an increase in the cost of production will pave way for an increase in the price of copper and a decrease in the cost of production will equally lead to a decrease in the price of copper. The cost of production in copper producing countries is normally influenced by other economic variables such as tax, cost of mining equipment and labor wage rates. An increase in one or more of these variables will affect the cost of production,
thus increasing the price of copper.

(I) Health of Home Building Industries

A commendable amount of the demands for copper come from home building industries. Copper is used by home building industries for wiring and piping. The health of Home building industries greatly influences the demand for copper. The demand for copper will normally increase when the home building industries are flourishing and decrease when home building industries are facing economic hardship. In line with the conventional relationship between demand and price, the price of copper will increase when home building industries are flourishing and it will fall during period when there is a low demand for the service of home building industries.

(J) Natural Disasters

Natural disasters constitute one of the significant copper price drivers. Natural disasters such as earthquakes and landslides are common in South America. Since the largest producer of copper are in this region, the supply of copper can be affected by Natural disaster. Natural disasters usually disrupt copper mining and destroy mining equipment. Thus, whenever there is natural disaster in any of the major copper producing countries, the supply of copper will decrease drastically and its price will increase sharply.

(K) Technological Developments

Positive developments in technology constitute one of the factors that have increased the demand for copper overtime. Due to incessant developments in technology, there has been an increase in the invention and new technologies whose production requires the use of copper. Whenever there is a new invention that requires the use of copper, the demand for copper will increase. This may consequently lead to an increase in the price of copper. It should be noted that the influence of a new product on the demand for copper depends on the relevance of the product to consumers on a global scale. If the new product is very relevant it will cause a remarkable increase
in the demand for copper, and vice versa.

Chapter Four

Factors Influencing the Price of Silver

Silver indubitably remains one of the most valuable and most useful metals in the world. It is extensively used in different economic sectors for one more reasons. Silver is used in manufacturing industries around the world for the production of high tech electronic appliances. It is also use in the medical industries as a disinfectant. Equally, silver is highly significant to the international economy as it has been one of the most enduring means of value storage for centuries. Just like other metals, the price of silver is determined by certain economic factors. Having a firm grasp of how these factors work will help traders and investors to make educated decision as regards the purchase and sales of silver.

Factors influencing the price of silver include: (A)
   Demand and Supply
As in the case of other metals, the force of demand and supply plays a significant role in determining the price of silver at a given time. The supply of silver in the world market is relatively stable even though its demand may fluctuate. This contributes to the status of silver as that precious metal whose value is always increasing. In this light, we can argue that demand is the main determiner of the price of silver in the global market. An increase in the demand for silver will equally result to an increase in the price of silver. There are various channel of demand that contributes to the price of silver in the global market. These channels include:

(i)   Industrial Demand

This channel accounts for demands for silver that come from manufacturing industries who use it for manufacturing high tech electronic appliances. Due to its high conductivity, silver is used in producing high tech electronics such as smart phones, flat screen televisions and solar panels. When the demand for these electronic devices and appliances are high, the demand for silver will increase as well, thereby leading to an increase in the price of silver in the global market. Industrial demand for silver covers more than 50% of the overall demand for silver in the world. In this vein, the demand for silver through this channel is a significant driver of silver price.

(ii)   Medical Demand

A commendable amount of the demand for silver comes from medical companies and industries that use it for manufacturing high tech medical equipment. Due to its anti-microbial and anti-bacterial property, silver is used extensively in medical firms as disinfectants. Demands from this channel also contribute to the relative increase in the demand for silver over time. Health is a primary issue. Thus, the demand for silver by medical industries is pretty significant.

(iii)   Investment Demand

Silver remains a high reliable source of storing value and purchasing power. It is considered to be a safe haven investment. As such, investors demand for silver to because of its enduring purchasing power and for profit making. Demands for silver in this channel come from both private and public investors. In fact, central banks around the world are known for buying and selling silver bullions in order to make profit and keep their economy going. The demand for silver for investments is usually high during economic instability. Consequently, the price of silver is usually high during periods of economic instabilities in the world.

It should be noted that the demand for silver in all these channels is largely determined by other economic factors (aside demand and supply) which shall be discussed in this chapter.

(iv) Jewelry Demand

This channel represents the demand for silver for the purpose of manufacturing jewelries. Increase in global demand for jewelries will increase the demand for silver in this channel and spike up the price of silver in the market. The demand for silver for the purpose of jewelry production is normally determined by the consumer spending rates and income.

(B) Inflation

Inflation plays a vital role in determining the price of silver at certain periods. Generally, inflation normally leads to a decrease in the value of paper currency and other currencies. Silver is a great hedge against inflation. Therefore, investors and central banks around the world normally demand for more silver in order to store value and purchasing power. In other words, investors and central banks normally demand for more silver during inflation in order to prevent the loss of value and purchasing power. This increase in the demand will automatically pave way for a sky high increase in the price of silver in the global market.

(C) Interest Rates

There is a negative correlation between the interest rates and the price of silver. That is, when interest rates increase the price of silver will decrease. Decrease in the price of silver when interest rates are high relates to the general decrease in the demand for silver by investors that usually accompany increased interest rates. When interest rates are high, most investors would prefer to invest in short-term interest paying investments
that has the tendency to yield high profit within short periods of time. The

general lack of interest in silver investments during this period will lead to a decrease in the demand for silver and the price of silver as well.

(D) Developments in Technology

The demand for silver is largely influenced by developments in new and existing technology. Technological developments usually lead to the discovery of new uses of silver which will eventually increase the demand for silver. For instance, developments in photovoltaic field have increased the demand for silver in recent times. Thus, it is clear that technological developments can lead to an increase in the price of silver.

However, it should be noted that technological developments can also lead to a decrease the price of silver. This manifests when technological developments facilities the discovery of substitute metals. The discoveries of substitute metal can affect the demand for silver negatively and cause its price to decrease. For instance, aluminum alloys which are acceptable as replacement for some cheap mirror is a product of technological developments.

More so, developments in technology relating to improved silver mining can increase the supply of silver, thus causing the price of silver to go down. The discovery of new silver mining technologies can make silver mining faster and easier. Speed and ease in silver production will in turn increase production rate and may cause the price of silver to decrease.

(E)Consumer Spending Rates and income

Consumer spending rates and income is a key determining factor to the price of silver in the market. Silver is not a primary commodity. Consumers usually demand for silver when there is an increase in their disposable income. The consumer's spending rate and income differs from one country to another. As such, consumer spending rate and income is one of the micro economic factors influencing the demand for silver. On the one hand, when job markets are stable and employment rate is high, there tends to be an increase in the demand for silver jewelries as the consumer spending rates and disposable income are generally high during this period. In this manner, the price of silver tends to increase during this period. On the other hand, when the job market is unstable and unemployment rate is high, their will a decrease in silver consumption as the consumer spending rates and disposable income are generally low during such periods. Logically, decrease in consumer spending rate and disposable income tends to decrease demand for silver and the price of silver as well.

(F) Strength of Dollar

Dollar is the global reserve currency. The strength of dollar tends to have a remarkable influence on the world's economy. Thus, the strength of dollar has the capacity to greatly influence the price of silver. There is an inverse relationship between the strength of dollar and the price of silver. Due to the leading status of dollar in the global economy, dollar depreciation may lead to a global value loss. Therefore, whenever dollar depreciates, investors and central banks around the world invest in commodities such as silver whose purchasing power is stable in order to prevent loss of value. This usually leads to a great increase in the price of silver.

On the other hand, an increase in the strength of dollar will reduce the demand for silver, thereby causing it price to decrease.

(G) Price of Crude Oil

There is a positive correlation between the price of crude oil and the price of silver. An increase in the price of crude oil will pave way for an increase in the price of silver. Generally, increase in the price of crude oil in the global market normally results into inflation. This tends to increase the demand for silver which is a reliable inflation hedger. In this light, the price of silver is usually high whenever the price of crude oil is high.

(H) Gold Price

Most of the factors influencing the price of both gold and silver are the same. As such, there is normally are remarkable similarities in the increase and decrease of gold price and that of silver price. An increase in the price of crude oil may guarantee the rise of silver price, and vice versa.

(I) Changes in China's Economy and Population

China is the largest consumer of silver in the world. Therefore, changes in the Chinese economy constitute one of the key determiners of the price of silver in the market. Positive changes in China's economy will increase the demand for silver, thereby causing an increase in the price of silver. Equally, negative changes in China's economy will cut down the demand for supply, thus causing the price of silver to decrease.

More so, the current increase in the population of China is likely to cause the price of silver to increase on a long run as increase in the population of China most likely to shoot up the demand for silver in the global market.

(J) Government Policies

Government policies from time to time play a significant role in determining the price of silver. Governments around the world have the power to make decisions regarding the production and buying of silver. These decisions may influence the price of silver directly or indirectly. For instance, if the government of a large silver consuming country such as China decides to place some restrictions on silver importation, it will automatically result into
a drastic decrease in the price of silver in the gold market.

Chapter Five

Factors Influencing the Price of Platinum

Platinum happens to be one of the elements known to man. Platinum is normally obtained as a byproduct of nickel and copper mining. However, despite its rareness, it happens to be one of the extensively used precious metals in the world. Platinum is generally used for both industrial and laboratory application. It is also among the most popular commodities for investors and traders in the world. Just like other precious metals, the price of platinum is very volatile. Its price depends on certain influencing factors which can directly affect its demand and supply. Investing or trading in platinum demand a clear understanding of how these price drivers work. Thus, let us take a close look at these price drivers.

   (A) Demand and Supply

The force of demand and supply is the basic factor that affects the supply of platinum and other precious metals in the global market. When the demand for a product is greater than its supply, the price of that product will increase. And when the supply of a product is greater than its demand, the price of the product will reduce. In the case of platinum, the demand for
platinum is usually greater than the demand for platinum because platinum is a very rare precious metal. This means that the price of platinum is usually based on how high or low the demand for platinum is. When the demand is high, the price of platinum will increase and when the demand for platinum
is low, the price of platinum will decrease. However, this does not mean that the supply of platinum does not have any effect on its price. If its supply reduces, it will result into a sharp increase in its price, and vice versa.

   (B)The South Africa Factor

South Africa is the largest producer of platinum. About 75 percent of platinum supply comes from South Africa and it also has about 95% of the global platinum reserve. South Africa is a developing country and a volatile emerging market. By this, we mean that the political atmosphere of South
Africa is not stable. This instability always has a strong influence on the

global supply of platinum. South Africa, just like other developing countries, is known for labor disputes, strike, instability in power and water availability and foreign currency instability. All this usually give way for a decrease in the supply of platinum, thereby causing the price of platinum to go up. For instance, the price of platinum increased uncontrollably in 2014 when workers of Lonmin, Anglo American platinum and Impala platinum all went on strike. For these reasons, it is advisable for investors and to look out for the situation of things in South Africa when dealing with platinum.

(C) Health of Automobile Industries

The automobile industries account for about 50% of the overall demand for platinum. Platinum is the least reactive and the densest metal. Due to this fact is used by automobile industries to manufacture catalysts converter which lowers emission in cars that have internal combustion engine. Decrease and increase in the sales and demand for automobiles in the world always have a significant effect on the price of platinum in the global market. When the demand for automobiles is high, the demand for platinum will increase and this increase will in turn increase the price of platinum in the global market. Contrarily, when the demand for automobile is low, the price of platinum will decrease in the global market.

Currently, the growth of Chinese automobile industries is one of the major factors driving the price of platinum in the global market. The price of platinum tends to be increasing due to the increase in the demand for platinum by Chinese automobile industries. In this light, investors and trader should look out for changes in China's economy which can in turn affect the demand for platinum by Chinese automobile industries. Buoyancy in
Chinese economy equates an increase in the demand and price of platinum, and vice versa.

(D) Technological Developments

Developments in technology are likely to have a negative effect on the price of platinum in the global market. The current increase in the production of electric cars due to technological improvements is likely to reduce the
demand for platinum in the market. In turn, this can result to a decrease in

the price of platinum because the automobile industry is the major consumer of platinum.

More so, developments in technology have paved way for the discovery of replacements for platinum in the production of catalyst converters. It has been discovered that the components of a catalyst converter can include about 20% to 50% of palladium. This could reduce the demand for platinum and eventually decrease the price of platinum.

Investors and traders should also note that the automobile industries are curiously in search of substitute metals. The price of platinum is very high. Thus, the automobile industries will give all it takes to find a suitable replacement for it in order to reduce the cost of production. For this reasons, it is advisable for investors to be on the look for developments in technology relating to the replacement of platinum in the automobile industries.

(E) Health of Jewelry Business

Jewelry industries account for a remarkable portion of global platinum demand. 20 years ago, there was little or virtually no demand for platinum by jewelry industries. However, recently, there has been a great increase in the demand for platinum by jewelry market. This increase is largely influenced by the increasing demand for platinum jewelries by Chinese consumers in the last 10 years. Moreover, there is currently a great increase in the demand for platinum jewelries by Indians. Thus, the demand for platinum by jewelry industries has greatly increase overtime. In 2016, the demand for platinum by jewelry industries accounts for about 31% of the overall demand for platinum in the global market.

In view of the foregoing, increase in the sales and demand for platinum jewelry will cause the price of platinum to rise. However, a fall in the sales and demand of platinum jewelry will equally cause a decrease in the price of platinum.

The sales and demand for platinum jewelry is most likely to be influenced by the economy of China and India. Positive developments in the economy of these countries will make the demand for platinum and the price of platinum to increase. Equally, economic breakdown in these countries will lead to a decrease in the price of platinum.

(F) Industrial Applications

Platinum is extensively use for a commendable number of industrial application. Platinum is used in the production on nitric acid which is used for producing explosives and fertilizers. More so, platinum is useful in the medical industries as it is used for in some biomedical applications such as dental alloys, crucibles and surgical instruments in surgical application. Increase in the demand for platinum by industries that need it for one or more industrial applications around the world will boost the demand for platinum and obviously increase its price. However, if the demand for
platinum by these industries decreases, the price of platinum can decrease as well.

Technological developments that relate to the invention and discovery of new products that requires platinum will increase the industrial demand for platinum and as well increase the price of platinum in the global market. For instance, the invention of fuel cell vehicles whose production requires more than the platinum used in combustion engine vehicles has increased the demand for platinum in the global market.

(G) Government Policies

Government policies can influence consumption and production of platinum in the global market. The government policies of major platinum consuming industries play a vital role in determining the demand and the price of platinum. For instance, if the government of a major platinum consuming country like China decides to restrict the importation of platinum, the
demand for platinum will drastically decrease. Consequently, it will lead to a decrease in the price of platinum in the global market as platinum will become relatively easy to purchase.

Moreover, government policy can influence the supply and production of platinum in the market. The major government to consider here is South Africa's government. As a developing country, there is generally political

instability in South Africa. South Africa is the world largest supplier of platinum. Thus, fluctuations in the politics of this country will normally affect the supply of platinum. Government policies relating to labor, exportation and tax rates in South Africa constitute a major factor in determining the price of platinum. For instance, if the government increases the tax rates on major platinum mining companies in South Africa, it will result into an increase in the cost of platinum production. Increase in the cost of production will definitely lead to an increase in the price of platinum. Policies relating to labor can also affect the supply and production of platinum. Unfavorable policies can lead to mining strike. Mining strike in South Africa will generally decrease the supply of platinum, causing the
price of platinum to fly up. (H)

Investment

The use of platinum for investment is relatively new. However, the demand for platinum by investors has recently increased. Investment demand for platinum accounted for about 11% of the overall global demand for
platinum. As such, increase and decrease in the rate at which investors invest in platinum tends to reflect on the price of platinum. Higher demands for platinum by investors can lead to a relative increase in the price of platinum, and vice versa. Investment demand for platinum is normally influenced by other factors such as interest rates, inflation and the strength of US dollar.

i.   Interest Rates

There is an inverse relationship between interest rates and the demand for platinum. That is, an increase in interest rates is equal to a decrease in the investment demand for platinum and a decrease in interest rates is equal to an increase in the demand for
platinum. Whenever interest rates are high, investors will generally reduce their investment in precious metals. Investors prefer to invest in interest paying investments when interest rates are high. This usually leads to a decrease in the general demand for
platinum. As a result of this, the price of platinum is most likely to go down when the interest rates are high.

ii.   Strength of US dollar

US dollar is the global reserve currency. As such, increase and decrease in the global economy. When dollar depreciates, it is common for investors and central banks around the world to increase their demand for precious metals in other to prevent loss of value and purchasing power. Platinum happens to be one of those precious metals that are used for insuring dollar depreciation. Hence, it is normal for the price of platinum to go high whenever dollar depreciates.

iii. Inflation

The effect of inflation on the price of platinum relates to the effect of the strength of dollar on platinum price. Platinum is one of the metals that are used as inflation hedgers. The common effect of inflation is currency devaluation. It is common for paper currencies to lose their value during inflation. As such, investors and central banks around the world usually demand for more platinum during inflation. Consequently, the price of platinum is normally high during inflation. When dealing with the price of platinum in the global market, the major country to consider is USA. This is as a result of the status of US dollar in the global market. The value of US dollar will fall when there is inflation in USA. This will in turn affect the global economy as US dollar is the global reserve currency. Thus, it is advisable for investors and traders to pay attention to economic trend in USA when dealing with platinum.

Conclusion

The price of gold, silver, platinum, copper and crude oil is very volatile. The price of these natural resources is generally determined by various non- economic and economic factors. However, the basic and direct driver of the price of these commodities is the force of demand and supply. All other influencing factors cannot affect the price of these commodities directly. Other influencing factors have an indirect influence on the price of these commodities because they can influence the demand and supply of these commodities in one way or the other. Thus, it is advisable for investors and traders to be well informed about the current status of the price influencing factors that we have discussed so far when dealing with any of these natural resources. Investors and traders should also be aware of the relationship
between the prices of each of these commodities in the global market.